RENDER

RENDER

POEMS   SACHIKO MURAKAMI

ARSENAL PULP PRESS
VANCOUVER

RENDER
Copyright © 2020 by Sachiko Murakami

ARSENAL PULP PRESS
Suite 202 – 211 East Georgia St.
Vancouver, BC V6A 1Z6
Canada
arsenalpulp.com

The publisher gratefully acknowledges the support of the Canada Council for the Arts and the British Columbia Arts Council for its publishing program, and the Government of Canada, and the Government of British Columbia (through the Book Publishing Tax Credit Program), for its publishing activities.

Arsenal Pulp Press acknowledges the xʷməθkʷəy̓əm (Musqueam), Sḵwx̱wú7mesh (Squamish), and səlilwətaʔɬ (Tsleil-Waututh) Nations, custodians of the traditional, ancestral, and unceded territories where our office is located. We pay respect to their histories, traditions, and continuous living cultures and commit to accountability, respectful relations, and friendship.

The following poems have been published in journals or anthologies: "Acknowledgments," *The Puritan* (Summer 2018); "An Internment," *Arc Poetry Magazine* 88 (Spring 2019); "Coda," "The Exact Nature of My Wrongs," "Following the Leader," "Mind Map of the Rendered World," and "Two Truths and a Lie," *Canada and Beyond: A Journal of Canadian Literary and Cultural Studies* Vol. 7 (2018) (Universidad de Huelva, Spain); "Community Healing" and "January," *Audeamus* 2017 (Massey College); "Field Research," *PRISM international* 57.1 (Fall 2018); "Forth" and "Performance Anxiety," *Hart House Review* 25; "Good God/Bad God," *NewPoetry.ca* and *The Best Canadian Poetry in English*, 2018 (Toronto: Tightrope Books); "He Said She Said," *POETRY* (December 2017); "A Tear Here," *Visual Verse*, Volume 5, Chapter 12.

Cover and text design by Jazmin Welch
Cover art by Jazmin Welch
Edited by Shirarose Wilensky
Copy edited by Jaiden Dembo
Proofread by Alison Strobel

Printed and bound in Canada

Library and Archives Canada Cataloguing in Publication:
Title: Render : poems / Sachiko Murakami.
Names: Murakami, Sachiko, 1980– author.
Identifiers: Canadiana (print) 20200203800 | Canadiana (ebook) 20200203819 |
    ISBN 9781551528274 (softcover) | ISBN 9781551528281 (HTML)
Classification: LCC PS8626.U72 R46 2020 | DDC C811/.6—dc23

For Manfredi

Render (*v. tr.*): to submit, as for consideration; to give or make available; to give what is due or owed; to give in return, or retribution; to surrender; to yield. To represent; to perform an interpretation of; to arrange. To express in another language or form; to translate. To deliver or pronounce formally; to cause to become; to reduce, convert or melt down, by heating.

Contents

STILL HERE

ENCOUNTER

Would you take a look at this
sweat held together
      by dream—the twined

frays of memory & history
twist of language and the form

a breath endures when you wake up

shaken, the fist
of trauma inches from

the hand of the word that would
submerge the Big Idea
      in bathwater

when the adults' argument
      drifts apart
      a *wah-wah* trombone
          ear canal awash with whoosh of escape

or come back
to the hum of today
where you could almost feel

what he feels, on the neighbour's porch
scrolling through his phone
checking for updates

on someone else's disaster

would you wait on the shore
a minute

passing just like my minute

your sea   my sea

there are many names for the ocean
where so many swim
frantic to reach the classroom

                    to take the test
                    teach the class
          find the almost-forgotten child

your anxiety   my anxiety
unclimbable towers
fall in a dream
and all structure

burns as memories
burn into sinew

your sinew

                    my throat
          drift apart
particular flotsam fills
our drowned lungs

          but none of it happened

the way I remembered
the moment I woke up

exhaling the dream
into your air

WHAT FIST IS THIS

regarding the end of here

MILK NIGHTMARE

Night training: a babe becomes accustomed
to the soothing taste of absence.
That same child grows up
and chooses a safe word: *milk.*

—

I say, *We need milk.* Everyone agrees
to my duplicity. I pantomime mouthfuls
of emptiness, one hand on the doorknob.

—

Need seems like the only memory
when it is present. First driving need,
then flat-out *more.* Hauled
to the brink of nightmare
conclusion, counting seconds.

Need. Need. Need.
Need. Need.

—

Need more.

—

Claw the dream dictionary
looking for citations
of *original thirst.*

Scrub the carpet's traces
of spilled milk.

Count every Tuesday you wake up,
thirsty, needful, sore.

DINNER TABLE

In the dream, the set table signals a romantic meal,
some fruitful beginning to some other dinner.
In the memory, it's the usual set-up, the weekday deal:

my place to the right of the father,
overcooked salmon, buttered rice, pitcher of
iced water. Mother missing. Didn't bother

(anxiety wmeal)

to mention the part about the dog's barbiturates,
how much, how little, the hatred of meal prep.
There is a note asking us to consider what

a life means. We haven't found out yet.
If I knew, would I have stopped the meal, felt
anything enough to hide my mouthfuls of apologies?

Instead, again, I mime drinking my milk
and taste the spray of panic seethe
through limbs like hot piss, stampeding full tilt

through the here and now, twitching beneath
the CBT techniques. I'm here. I'm there. Something's wrong
with my chosen procedure. Retrieve fork from between teeth,

chew the flat, unreasonable number. Burning panic of two,

left at the table. The dream meant I could learn how to fully feel.

I've lost my appetite for this. May I please be excused.

THANATOPHOBIA I

[handwritten annotations: "very intellectualized" / "(they're so chilly)" / "— prose lacks more — clichéd personification / really fresh / intensity"]

Death rides with her in the back seat of the Civic over the Port Mann again, where an easy earthquake could ungird bridge steel, send the family down into the Fraser, the weight of the river more than a little girl could kick against. She holds her breath from Surrey to PoCo.

Death yawns, trying to trigger a sympathetic opening. She grasps at lungful of air like it's the last thing she'll ever have.

Despite Death yelling, continually, *Boo!*

[handwritten: "why "n" here but not here?!"]

All those knives, drifting in dishwater. Razors in Halloween candy. Broken traffic lights.

Death nudges her chin up to the sky. Acid rain, Soviet bombs, asteroids. Death shows her the size of his hands, which are as big as planets, as thought.

Death squeezes her heart once she learns what a heart is, and how it regularly fails.

Boo! Boo! Boo!

[handwritten: "trying to switch registry but it's untophisticated / but it's heavyhanded."]

Every night, Death sits on the side of the bed, its red grimace hovering, fingers tracing the outline of her nightie.

A hand finds its way under, to chest, through spine, deeper. Omits the hand, the nightie, the present.

She tries sleeping in the bathtub, the closet. Somewhere he won't find her.

Death suggests words that propel her to the living room, where she stands, gasping, out of grammar. *It's. Here. Again.*

She's ignored her for the most part, until the kitchen floor gets dirty. *You don't notice this filth,* a stain no one can see. Then a car is driven away, a vow never to return. In retaliation, a sister packs two small suitcases, but she goes back to the closet. Counts hangers.

A return and an absence unspoken. A pizza is ordered.

Other days, things are broken: cupboards, dishes, pets, her future. Everything around her but her, in the closet, sucking the corner of the familiar.

Death can't find her in the back of the closet. Just kidding! Death can find her anywhere.

There is nowhere the jagged edge of life is that he isn't. She waits at the bottom of this shallow breath until

she doesn't mind

Death won't shut up about the knives that could cut an artery, now that she knows about arteries.

Psychologists are called. *I think she's going to kill me* is intoned. *She's obsessed with the knives.*

Her will comes up against irrevocable bridges, knives, the purr of engines as cars pull out of driveways.

What are you worried about?

It just feels like I'm going to die, she fumbles. *One day, I know. But at any time.*

Death leans against the door frame, amused.

Her will a silent chant that keeps all beloved arteries whole.

What do you have to be worried about?

Death hums along to the deafening song, *I am leaving, I am leaving, but the fighter still remains.* She wakes and walks towards the living room, where a crumpled form is a bad dream.

Bags are packed. Bags are unpacked. Things are done to keep busy.

The closet is flung open. There's a recording device in there, maybe. The source of the voices.

There are noises until there is no noise but the TV.

But no one gets off that easy.

AN INTERNMENT

An emptiness placed here, by the state.

Soft teeth crumble into boxed dust, carted to Ontario, of all places.

I'm going to turn this car around, I swear.

Filial hunger, filial debt, filial panic disorder.

In the rented house, we searched for secrets as though an object could contain truth.

Instead he arrives disguised in dreams.

Some other condo, some other wife.

I'm leaving. I'm sick of your shit.

—

I'm sick of your shit credit score.

Cemeteries, with their enduring monuments, their old-money teeth.

Or: two child-size suitcases packed full of hunger, shoved in the closet, farther back than therapy can reach.

There where the question hits lockbox.

Then there's this old pick.

Floss, ribbons of floss. Excessive floss. Enough to hang yourself with.

Scrape until something bleeds.

—

Scrape until something bleeds cash.

Scratch cards a whispering accordion. Unsung lotto jingle.

You think you have a home until the landlord rings.

The fallow field behind the junked cars, the junked cars beyond the house, the house, burning.

Even that insurance policy covers someone else.

Or: an infant feels a draft, and settles back into hunger, coiling herself into the genetic sequence.

Until a man shudders out his loss into a mother.

She unravels to make room for him.

—

She unravels to make room for his anger.

The more empty spaces inside her, the more soft places for his hurt to land.

She opens again in a gesture of more.

You are nothing. You're on your own.

I can't do this without you. Get out of here.

—

Come here. I need to tell you the thing
he forgot to tell me about, a gap
like this old, broken tooth, like
the gnaw of ancestral hunger or
some unexplained dry plate
you spend your dreams
trying to ignore. The same emptiness.
The same state as before.

YOU HAVE MEMORIES

remember your **end** ere the end

FORTH

Froth of summer, the gorgeous unhinging.

Men rupture sweet hangover dusk.

Invention slip-knots you, mother of midnights.

Stars bite into your lip and you wish knives.

Cuts of indecision, beaded promise.

Hustle past present, a chintzy excuse, or hurtle towards bland reality's dopamine curl.

Then your leavings gather in eddies around you. Those continual last chances.

You brown into bits, reorganized by the dream.

Tawny air escapes the immaterial. Molecules march from you.

You lapse from child to pitiful fantasy in a matter of minutes.

Somewhere in a snowstorm, flakes melt the subjunctive mood.

The begin again begins again. Carries you with it.

THANATOPHOBIA II

Death smirks. *You really ought to cool it with the drugs.* Then slips out the door.

Sprawled in the aftermath of herself, her evening the size and shape of her heart, the length of an artery, the width of a child's closet. One foot on the swaying bridge, an errant knife in her hand.

Calling to him. Praying, even.

Texting threats.

An ambulance arrives, its lights off.

What seems to be the problem, miss?

BREATHER

Flame on tongue as real as a hallucination.
You wake and you are no dragon. You are as real
as any patient in a psych ward.

The day on par with the expected result. Blank walls and
blank walls. All metaphors stop at the nurses' station.

On a smoke pass, stoop to listen to the flat earth's warning couched in silence,
rib cage held against the flame of interpretation.

Call your boss: you're not coming in today.
Then return reality to the nurses' station. Sealed in a plastic bag.

Act crazy so it's not just a spa day.

—

Constant and luminous peril leaps from moment to moment, throat to throat.

Subliminal or sublingual to modestly salubrious.
The false sense of reality, this non-movement
of the mind through the mouth. Everything that can open, opens,
save one locked gate.

Turn away and return to the fumble through diction and let
the hangover dissolve into silence.

—

Unwrapped lust, a float unstrung
from the trudge of parade, drifting.

At first it looks like freedom, but
that's going to choke a gull, eventually.

—

Prowling the hallways of unfamiliar condos in a torn sundress.
Blank walls. Blank
hurtle towards the end of the night.

Godiva in the back, Ichabod in the front. Behind the closed door, a million wives.

—

Who are we kidding. You're nobody's wife.

Nobody needs to twitch towards family.

Not even a bit.

—

It could have ended there:

Bottom as in the *end of doing harm*. *Bottom* as in *no further passage.*

Scraping at earth as though there were a way to hell.
You keep digging because you hope
there might be a glint of violence
that will tear you open the way

God tears some open. A cut of red.
A crack in the wall. But this time
there's nearly

no morning at all.

ACKNOWLEDGMENTS

the edge blurred

                                                        face, dissolving

lorazepam, memory

                        oil gathered on surface
                            a filmic

voice saying
I had wanted
this for a long

                        grey sky, never reflected
                            a storm

behind shadowed
curtains, talk

                                        to two different sponsors
                                        about the nature of consent
                                        in a blackout

gulf of throat
between *then* and *now*

                          turns ankle as a boot sinks
                                into water

filled space between
he and
a white rail
and he

                              stifles reflection

of *I'm too fucked up*
to drive home

                                          or *I need to sleep*

                          in dream city, built
between *he* and
who holds

                        a broken woman below

her, circling the city with

                                                    your conduct,
                                          not the conduct of others

listed
in the thank-yous
under *all the people I may have forgotten*

                                          or if he was in a blackout

                              between my legs

a dream
of the friends
preserved in the photograph
of what happened before

                                          you'll never know if you gave

                              the dark voice

a dream
my writing
was better than this

                                                body listening to my body's

story not
worth preserving

                        in a dream

I put the girl to bed

                   and watch until
                   he leaves

                                        whoever lived here

                                        still lives here

MIND MAP OF THE
RENDERED WORLD

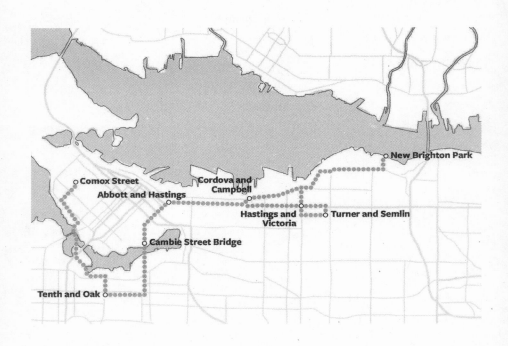

COMOX STREET

I have amnesia. I come to and I am in an unfamiliar house watching a touching movie with strangers. I am surprised that it is so moving because it is a Disney after-school special. The lead male is attractive in a late-teenage way. Dark hair, rebellious, dangerous, but ultimately, he cares deeply for the female lead. I get up to go after the movie ends and the strangers all snicker at me. I can't find my shoes. I get increasingly upset that I don't know where or when I am. The really heartbreaking moment is when they tell me it is November, not July, as I had thought. Apparently, they had found me on a slut-review website. I came over and fucked all of them in turn. I remember nothing.

TENTH AND OAK

I am a man manipulating other men into giving me drugs. Lots of people are living in my house, using it as a movie set. I am high among familiar men, some of them mentors. I wake up, still dreaming, and find photos on my phone. Some are sexualized photos of children. I am confused and horrified. An investigation begins. We are, rightly, charged with child abuse.

CAMBIE STREET BRIDGE

I am in a fantasy land where I feel peace. I perform an impassioned monologue about sunflowers to a swirling prophetess. She agrees to let me stay, and implies that my path will be paved with sunflowers, but I will have to slay the dragon. I set out on my journey. Then, without warning, long before the appointed time, the dragon descends. It is metallic, cruel, mocking. It tells me to go back where I came from. I try my hand at bravery and it eats me. I slosh around in its stomach. When I escape, I charge it again. It picks me up in its teeth and flies very rapidly with the intention of slamming me into a wall.

CORDOVA AND CAMPBELL

I decide to work for my father at his store. He sits, as usual, in his office, watching a squirrel video on his computer that in the dream is erotic. He calls his business partner to confirm my rate of pay: nineteen dollars per hour, which is four dollars more than he would pay my sister. I try to explain that she won't be able to do it because she has her own job now. I am stuck in a family business, unhappy, but my father is happy, so I take my place at his side.

NEW BRIGHTON PARK

I am dining with fashionable people. My water glass is full of frog spawn. I try to get some fresh water, but it comes out of the tap sloppy and full of more frog spawn. Someone has cursed my water supply. I can barely choke down the slimy water, but I am dying of thirst, so I must keep trying.

HASTINGS AND VICTORIA

I win $25,000 for a really good speech.

TURNER AND SEMLIN

When we arrive at the airport, my sister and I get in line for the bus. We realize at the last minute that we neglected to buy tickets. She prints some out at a machine, which unspools a rambling passage from a badly written erotic novel. Everyone else has tidy, trimmed tickets and we have this obvious mess of paper. I don't understand, but my sister is looking at me knowingly. It is, apparently, from a piece of writing attributed to me online, which we must present to the authorities to verify my identity. I am livid. Why would she pick this, clearly not mine, when so much of my actual writing is on the Internet?

ABBOTT AND HASTINGS

I visit my mother in a high-rise shelter where she is sleeping because in her own place the voices keep her awake. I try to reason with her, but she doesn't believe me. I lie down with her and she curls into my hollow spaces like a child. I am very tired, but I can't sleep. I am worried they will tow my car. I am worried about bedbugs. I go get us lattes from the hipster coffee shop downstairs. It is hard to find my way back, because I am in unfamiliar territory, and so tired.

HOW FAR INTO THE FUTURE CAN YOU SEE

from inside a box of cloud-shaped fear
through a million tiny poked holes vs.

you with ten fingers, a singular dumb plug
the breadth of the present or its seepage vs.

all the bodies hauled through mist, rising up
from plywood boxes like regretted texts vs.

you with semen drying in your hair, the hotel door's
pneumatic seal, its definite and final click vs.

the view from inside the feral cat,

through matted fur, inside her furious

sore, her mewling sex,

pawing at the door

vs.

a piteous drift
downriver through the unknown reeds
away from mother

vs.

twenty boxes of books in cold storage vs. the silverfish
form that will not hold

vs.

a calendar appointment

even a tentative appointment

FIELD RESEARCH

I talk about my dreams like there is some factual evidence that will survive the trauma of waking and realizing the truth of my life: its plodding linearity, the plumb line that follows a bullet's path to the next day, and the day after that.

I'm told I should stay present. I'm told there is safety in the out-breath, that there is a space between thought and thinker I would see if only I held still long enough to measure the distance.

Between here and Vancouver, most of a continent. Between a mother and daughter, a sinew stretching city blocks. Pluck it and it twangs at the same frequency as the knotted trapezius, the first note of a dirge you've been humming since early childhood.

Check her breathing. Prepare a plausible story for why you're here, a lie you will tell to tomorrow. When the doctors arrive they will wave the usual instruments over our lives, listening for signals of the past. When does chronic bronchitis become a child you can name, a treatable condition?

My out-breath her in-breath, a chain that follows generations backwards to the first woman leaning over, heaving out sorrow into a man's empty bed. I lie down with my mother on a single mattress. Lions reach into me, following the lines I laid out for them, on her dresser.

We sleep for days, a litany of Tuesday mornings marching past window, facing courtyard, a place where exhaled sleep gathers. I dream I read her diary and uncover all the secrets that will answer all the questions. I stand poised and ready to ask.

DIG IN

surrender

THE EXACT NATURE OF MY WRONGS

Evidential hip won't swing
through the full arc

of the present moment

fulcrum stuck in time
when the locomotive urge towards the future

meets the bound and gagged girl

stop here, now
take a photo for the archives

gather the weight of her grief
and take her to your bed, then

friend her on Facebook and leave her
to her walk of shame

picture this: Princess Street, four a.m.
a girl limps and considers

joining a yoga class
and then pukes again

keeps walking towards
the future with its

endless possible outcomes they keep
telling her will they keep telling

her will the present open as a hip
in asana or will it seize as it did

when the dark closed around her
that first night and every

night she woke again in the same
sick truth of her immutable body

or will she stay in the

track of a sigh
and rehash her story

what it was like
what happened
and what it's like today

FOLLOWING THE LEADER

1. A game moves forward from failure, starts the process of *we*.

2. Feel free to assume a few things about yourself based on your shadow's gait.

3. Close your eyes and try to copy me.

4. Now tell me how that felt.

5. The humiliated lead the humiliated, standards limping.

6. I move my hand *thus* and my mind moves with it, for once.

7. Without depth, I mimic dots on a page.

8. I can hear him walking, and I want to fall in step. I am mostly this scenario.

9. We make brunch plans. I've always hated brunch.

10. Let's go over that one more time.

11. Am I doing this right? Are you?

12. Sure, I'll be your footnote. Where should I stand?

THANATOPHOBIA III

He hints he might call her.

They agree to stop seeing other people.

He goes out one night, comes back with a familiar face on.

She waits for him to get in the shower, and then scours for evidence.

Turns out pockets, looking for a black hole. Finds it.

She and Death breathe a unanimous sigh of relief.

COMMUNITY HEALING

In the time it takes to reach
the end of an hour

to not say
the Lord's Prayer

I do not reach for
the man's fingers

do not speak
in the silence's

rail against
silence: the wrath

of the men
and their armfuls

of hand-drawn
valentines

when my ex
nears and his whispers

tickle the lobe
of my conviction

which upon waking
seems to mean

art might save me.
Art never saves me.

THE FIELD OF ARTIST'S RENDITIONS

At the edge of the property, those shadows
wisps beyond earshot, half-seen,
scribbled in mist. Figures risen, possibility.
Men I could have encountered
all those days I never left the house.

All those nights I did,
when every noise that tore through
collapsed into one urgent call: *Come to the woods.*
Put out like an anxious cat.

Sometime later, I describe a man's face
and charcoal scrapes against parchment,
finds the hard line of shadow,
small placid mouth, tug of smirk
leaves me here among the ghosts, circling.

Then the light glints and fades: only the crack
of birch branch, held breath,
then the light glints and fades: only the crack
leaves me here among the ghosts, circling.

Small placid mouth, tug of smirk
finds the hard line of shadow,
and charcoal scrapes against parchment.
Sometime later, I describe a man's face,

put out like an anxious cat,
collapsed into one urgent call: *Come to the woods.*
When every noise that tore through
all those nights I did,

all those days I never left the house.
Men I could have encountered
scribbled in mist. Figures risen, possibility
wisps beyond earshot, half-seen
at the edge of the property. Those shadows.

A STRANGER'S JUST A FRIEND YOU HAVEN'T MET YET!

A man I haven't met awake

A man whose name I don't remember

A man with whom I may have slept

A man I knew in high school, maybe

A man I dated but never met

A man I never met

A man I never met sober

A man who never emailed me back

A man I never want to meet

A man I never meant to meet

A man whose face I don't remember

A man who reminds me of my father

A man who reminds me of my ex

A man who reminds me of my deficiencies

A man who laughs when I can't remember

A man who doesn't have to run after me

A man I ran after but never caught

A man behind the door, I'm sure of it

TWO TRUTHS AND A LIE

I loved him more than I loved poetry. I loved cocaine more than I loved poetry. When I told him I loved him, I meant *I love you more than cocaine.*

When I was with him, I forgot about cocaine: this was the crux of my love. I thought of using cocaine when he asked me to leave. I thought of leaving while I was using.

I used and lied about it. I lied about lying. All cocaine users are liars.

I threatened to use after he left. I used after he left. He found me after I had used after he left: he was cool about it.

Cocaine is its own poetry, if by poetry you mean a skilfully crafted web of lies. I transcribed my lies as poetry. Every word of this is a lie.

GOOD GOD/BAD GOD

HONESTY

I try to sneak my god in, which obviously won't work. She is not a sneaky god.

REGRET

My dead father acquires a god. The only evidence of their relationship is the backyard full of shit.

RESPONSIBILITY

I am to take out someone else's god for a walk, and someone else's child from school. I wander off on a journey, alone.

FEAR

On retreat in the country, the locals and their gods mock me and my god. We barricade ourselves against their threats.

RAGE

Near a sidewalk crowded with god walkers, I am stuck in a car with my angry, unleashed god.

LOVE

Some young gods fit in the palm of your hand. Some have definite heft. All are cared for by others.

INTELLIGENCE

My god is prone to attacking children. We walk with purpose into a schoolyard.

SHAME

I take my god to an improbable park. She finds the only mud puddle and rolls in it.

REDEMPTION

My dead god is waiting for me, near the pool.

PERSONAL RESPONSIBILITY

Technical difficulties stall the curtain
and the audience shifts, restless as ever.

I worry I'll disappoint the crowd again,
what with these hand-stitched suits, this hopeless endeavour,

and then the understudy comes, all glitz and pearls,
to threaten my place in the social order.

The script I'm given reveals my lines. *Fourth Girl:*
enter stage left, when everything's over.

My perception of myself is beyond excuse.
I text the doctor to confirm my disorder.

On stage, Third Girl spins a story of abuse
to appease the audience a little longer.

I turn to the woman who has recently quit the drink
and in the washroom I describe what it means to be sober

until the boss comes in, tells us to scrub sinks.
It's not always like this, I weakly assure her.

When it's my turn I clip-clop out in my obvious gait,
then leave, disgusted, in the midst of my surrender.

No one's shocked I fail to play it straight.
The star steps to the curtain with her future about her.

There's no denying it. I'm a loser.
I reach, half-hearted, for the nearest man.

At least I didn't run to the nearest boozer.
At least I have this weak-ass plan.

I'M DYING

In search of a cool place
to prevent my mood
from spoiling

my ambition
thrown in the back of the cortex
among the mustards

Ping! My failure
versus everyone else

throwing back their heads
and laughing *Ping!* again

My lunch lacks
the requisite photo-ready friends

No one hears
a murmured word
caught dumb

tongue rolled
to the perilous edge

of how close
I get to a drink
without dying

CODA

what does trauma do

it insists

what does it insist

a sentence of a vagueness
        that is violence is authority and a mission
                stumbling and also certainly also a prison

relieve me of the bondage of your sentence
that I may better form a will

grant me the serenity to accept
the difference

between *now* and *then*

then the seize of fear shuts down the machine
of language, the hurtle towards the end of the sentence

left hanging
here in the exact nature
of my wrongs

THE BIG ONE: FIELD NOTES

Searched Google Earth to locate the exact spot: came up against limits.

Optic nerve bristles in panic,

neural havoc I snorted or swallowed or tried to sleep off,
weak little dendrites and so many infinite, failing leaps. Click

around the map: there's the spot, or maybe a bit farther
north, no.

Shift tactics to the book by the bed,
Jung's ideas about dreams

which I'll get to,
one day—

Started at the bay, where the scenery eclipses the self.

Conjure the safest space imaginable
in order to endure

twenty more minutes

and articulate
the world

rushing in
through the open
throat

Described the environs in detail in order to be able to more easily recall the space when I needed it.

One bed, two duvets

After an hour's swim, a dog in repose

Tea cooling in an oversized, chipped mug

Open window, fir and cedar conducting wind

Drifting through the imagined Active Pass

a real rowboat full of rapists

I couldn't explain what I meant when I said, "Poetry is bodiless."

When I am here in
a different relationship

where the imagined body
feels real pain

I narrated the experience to a woman who is a mystery to me.

Limbs tingling.

      Stay with it. Keep telling me.

Strong tingling, like they are waking up from being asleep.

      Can you keep talking?

It's not changing. I feel like I shouldn't say anything

                        unless it changes

Woke up again in terror, not at the dream but at the prospect of never waking again.

Do you sequester your fear of the Big One
in the bone made silent by the muscle tensed around it
in protection against the day the tension releases all at once as
an earthquake shatters condo glass
rain down while you wonder
what you will do now
that everything is as broken
as you always
suspected it was

or do you just try to not think about it

Do you miss Vancouver?

[straight, decent roads
lead to my dealers: Smithe & Beatty,
Nelson & Burrard, my foot on the gas,
brake, gas while I chant, *Turn around,
turn around*, but the benzos
render this fight
no fight at all and the
road pulls me
along until

I get
what's
coming
to me]

Yes, of course

In my relapse dreams I am in Vancouver,

hiding a bundle in my shirt like
I've been picking roadside blackberries

the line for the bathroom a Möbius strip
of disinterested friends

my reasoning too circuitous to figure out
how to get all of what I'm hiding up my nose before I'm caught

When I wake I'm sober.
I think. Yes.

The important part of dreaming
is that I wake up clean

& drenched in sweat

Bad day again today.

Waiting for the Big One,

              some other she

              crouched in my upright stance

who holds the key

              that unlocks the door

that maintains in stasis

            the dark room where

the blank-faced man jumps out

                and says, *Surprise*

What I want: a thread to unwind through the labyrinth

What I'm given: a long-form census

Just a break from being me, for one day

When you say *freedom*
                    you have in mind a horse

driven by wild instinct
                    galloping down Main Street

through the bewildered throng
                    to the desert beyond

when in this reality, your desert-life
                    is all thirst & midges

and in the time since you moved to Toronto
          the city has rewritten
          most of your memories
          and Main Street doesn't look at all how you remember

UPON WAKING

render render render render render render

I RETURN TO THE ISLAND
OF MY FATHER'S CHILDHOOD

I am heading inland from the safety of Long Harbour
with the body in the back seat wrapped in linen

ready for the family cremation.
The body of the island is wrapped in dusk,

ready for the night's throttle.
Where their burned house was, a new house.

Slip through family history, a snag in the shoulder
where the memory was: a burned memory.

Slip through the corridor, a snag of estranged aunts,
and reach the end where a wail starts

to expand his legacy into the air.
I reach the switch to start the conveyor belt,

and hand over his body to his heirs,
aunts who harry the darkness, busy as ever.

Where does the tunnel lead? I ask my sister,
who carries the darkness, weary as ever.

Where do dreams lead? asks my sister,
an echo as I enter the tunnel

clanging reverb on the flat road to nowhere,
heading inland from any safe harbour.

BREAKING AND ENTERING

In Iceland with my sister in a cave,
both tricked into a sleep by foreign ghosts,
the details ... vague. We escape or retreat
when our mother comes, keys jangling,

to guard against the fear. It's odd of her
to cross the ocean without being asked.
She settles in and hints she needs some help
to score a scrip. *This should have been a sign,*

I scribbled on the page while waiting in
the Toronto Western psych emerg
above the noted score of Biles's gold
floor routine (15.966), and

the words I caught and saved from air that night:
This city's full of pimps, johns and dealers
and all the bad people. Fuck this. Fuck you.
I shouldn't have worn mascara, although

it's possible this last line came from me.
I carry words from then to now to stop
from slipping underground into that empty,
dark, motherless cave. *Load of good that did.*

I've no notes from the triage interview,
which they performed behind a metal door.
They must have written *voices urging harm*,
since *self-harm* is coded as a *crisis*,

while *psychosis* can be treated at home,
by family. *I can't imagine how*
this feels, no doctor ever said to me.
I drove home alone, and that night I dreamed

of an anxious girl who speaks pain aloud:
each trauma she has ever had, save one.
I take my notes, and read to her from my
prescription pad. It doesn't soothe. Not yet.

She says, *I want my fucking phone*. We want
to hear the music of the keys, although
we know better this empty, soundless want,
no mother, no one come to take us home.

WHOSE COOKIES ARE WE TALKING ABOUT?

She's caught with her hand in the cookie jar,
sweet smear on midnight lip. A friend's hand
hovers on the light switch. One of them feels bad;
one crumbles silence and whispers the truth:

These cookies are neither low-carb nor gluten-free.
Whether or not she is actually my friend or
the man crouched in the bad feeling is my father
may never resolve into truth. What can you do

with cookie crumbs that lead—where? The tenant's
basement bedroom, a bathtub? A friend shares her story
and across my face a shadow of bad feeling unfurls
its blindfold panic when a hand brushes truth. What would

happen if I ate all the cookies I wanted, really?
My friend, would you like one, too? My therapist asks,
What does "feel bad" feel like? I describe
a sensation that is lodged somewhere near the truth

stuck in my throat, like a cookie eaten in secret.
Here in the kitchen, I have no friends. I am held
by a bad feeling that starts in the dream,
ends choking on a half-woken truth.

DREAM SISTER

Sister, what are you doing in my dream
again, relapsing on my behalf? Why aren't
you taking this relapse more seriously?
Why were you partying the night before we
have to move? Isn't this *my* cocaine, am I
not meant to hide it in my bra? What if
there's death waiting at the bottom of that?
Never mind, we need to pack. Do you want
this? Do you *really* want this? Should I get
rid of it? Can I keep it? Why aren't you
listening to anything I say?

———————————————————

I can't answer if I'm not listening. I can't
keep it. I can't get rid of it. I want it. I *want*
it. Death is waiting, but today's ungodly
reprieve keeps me here. It is my cocaine.
The party goes on inside me long after
everyone has left. It isn't a relapse because
I didn't ever stop. This is my relapse dream.
This is my behalf.

SLEEP PAST CRISIS, AGAIN, UNTIL

you arrive at another crisis.

Drag the dead father
home from Kazakhstan.

Crack a joke
that hits awkward angles.

Eat your relapse meal
in full view of his rotted body.

Pour oil in the hole
as per his instructions.

Never mind how slick
the regret.

All we need to do now
is get him in the shower!

I CHOOSE YOU

The young men mock me for lurking
in a public garden. That's the *wrong garden,*

idiot. Nothing spawns there. I wield my shovel,
a tool to cleave strangers' melons. Maybe, I insinuate,

I'm making graves for my dead Pokémon.
Maybe all they see are my empty hands.

They have no idea what I do with myself
in my spare time, that this

halved and hollowed fruit will keep a beast
that cries only its own name:

Terror, Terror. Maybe we're not in training
for the same thing. Fingers numb from the effort.

Men disperse or scatter. I feed a high-level terror
candy, made of ground-up, weaker terrors.

At the boundary of my vision, more men,
more terror, unless, as before,

I'm inventing these figures to combat
solitude. That summer, I logged

over a hundred klicks in search of—
Well, I walked to the lake, at least, where

everyone else caught more relief than me,
what with their battery packs, their amiable chatter.

All this is a distraction from your eventual death,
offers my nine-year-old nephew,

standing somewhere nearby, his possible futures
held in his fist, faintly glowing.

ENOUGH

It's my party, and all I do is fail
to accurately count the silken limbs of my guests
in a sullen and whispered summation. *One, two.*
Wallflowers ten deep align like constellations,
flaunting the mystery of their auspicious births.
An uncharted neuroscientist slides into the equation,
drops hope in my mouth. *Three, four.*
Pills dissolve into the compulsion
to offer the same hospitality to all the young women,
to stroke thighs without mentioning it. If no one notices,
it means our ruse is a success. His low voice assures me
the pursuit of pleasure precludes happiness. If I can eat this plate
of canapés without anyone seeing, *five, six*, it means there is enough.
I describe my dopamine binges, *seven, eight, nine.*
For the mirrors, I perform a good cry. I've lost count
of the connections made without my intervention.
The algorithm marches on to produce the expected result,
beaded sweat recorded upon waking.

STILL HERE

re-enter the rendered

PERFORMANCE ANXIETY

I read the future
by guessing at characters
caught in the glare
of my dying laptop
moonlighting as
my next grant-funded
ahem on
my to-do list marked by
excuses uncalled for
by the dozen or hundred
obvious elisions
that cleave the throaty
midnight hard drone
over emoji spilled
from the gaped mouth
of a liar who knows
the truth's a mistake

HE SAID SHE SAID

I swallowed the sweet thing in a dream. I woke up heavy.
I said, aloud, *What's the matter with you, Dad?*
As if language were a refuge. You taught me
to run to/from only moving one frantic eye.
Something stitched, so back to the argument.
Stop seeing what's the matter with me.
Ghosts are better than reanimated fathers, and
it is more acceptable to steal from the ether.
When you said, *We take matters into our own hands,*
I stopped starting the day with a ritual. No more
ecstasy pulled from a fluted throat. Return to the
bland, daily mouthlessness. I said,
Here are all the wrongs I was told to address to you.
Then the driftwood settled on your ashes. *Well,* you said.
As if there were presence enough in me to notice
the aha finger-snap announce its failure.
I guess I'm less angry, now that you don't exist
where I am left to a singular silence. Whistling nothing
like wind through fistulae. As if I were here without
you, with only the sound of these walls.

FIRST TRY OR FAILURE

it comes, a gush of mirror

of mirror of what I resembled yesterday
reconstituted on the horizontal axis

the scatter-dot evidence
the dread of the form's
algorithmic

tissue, an abstraction of she,
as in, nothing flushes under scrutiny
more than *she*

presupposes nothing but grief or possible endless
first trimesters strung together

mothballs, mothballs, mothballs

on the sill under the same sun as yesterday's
still or demonstrable now

or misgiving or
almost nothing
worth mentioning

the lack of gerund
the sound of the sea

or the empty sea or
no sea sounds as empty as this

sounding through the appropriate way
to bring up emptiness

downward?
solitary?
fast

intelligent flush
and doing
despite data

delivered under
the coursing
fact: whatever

they said the moment
might surrender,
it's all blood
all now

THERE'S NOTHING THERE

the slack
gel slides
the dry bed

sound
of the
wanted

held to hear
hoofbeats
no sounds

sea sounds
as empty as this
gel on empty

sound bed
of the wanted
throat

sounding
throat sounds like
the empty

way said there's
nothing
to say

the slack
surface of
there's nothing

there see
sounds
nothing

sea
sounds
there

nothing
there
of nothing

not in
the here in
the slack sea

TRY

it comes, a voice in mirror

in mirror of what I am here, now
reconstitute in the library   of all places

their voices' evidence
the call of their bodies'
algorithmic

tissue, an expression of she
as in, nothing flushes under scrutiny
more than *she*

presupposes the sound of possible endless
first tries strung together

voices, voices, voices
behind me holding me
still demonstrable she

and misgiving or almost
a sound worth listening to

the lack of
the sound of she

she

or no—she sounds empty, now

sounding through the appropriate way
to bring up emptiness

outward
community
fast
intelligent flash

and doing
despite data

delivered under their coursing noise:

whatever they said the moment
might surrender
it's all here
all now

JANUARY

Today you make use of silence
and yet the dark winter curls around your will
like an old friend you wish would leave
but finally accept in your skin like the knowledge
that this pool was the site of some kid's death
while you swim as though anyone
were after your insufficient breath
and a childhood that looms in every second-guess
of your insufficient breath that swims
as though anyone were after
its death. You catch sight in this pool of some kid's
knowledge of motion, and accept
you will have leave, and then the old friend
curls around your will and lets dark winter
make use of your silence today

THAT FEELING WHEN

he speaks and
everyone listens while

he ushers me out of his bed
over and over
and over my
skin's
electric scatter
says again that

it's
going to get bad
before it gets
better
and it's not
going to get
better while
I come to
with
him inside me

and he's
always inside me

when he speaks, the audience
responds with
polite applause
or maybe thunderous applause or
raucous, knowing, in-on-it applause

I wouldn't know
I wasn't there

I paid for my performance
half in shame, half

of a sentence that crawls back into silence
and widens into

every wordless scrape of failure

funnelled into a single half-truth
that marches
                    across this page, meeting other

                    bits of blind faith

                    trailing off into

                              wherever

                                                  how exactly
                                                  shall I make
                                                  art from this silence

can someone please send me
the full list of attendees
so I can decide well in advance
whether it's safe
to carry this weight
into a room of strangers
who may or may not
know you still
kick against
my gut and
the pain
could
make
me

almost nobody

for a minute

I'm sorry I can't remember
the exact nature of the incident, so I can't say *yes* he is my

(he hovers there
in the space between *what i can say* and *libel*

a fucking artless nuance

clutching his name
like a golden statuette)

In my first year of sobriety
because it would not injure him or others

I say
I'm sorry I showed up at your house drunk

he says
almost nothing

it both is and is not a specific *he*

who sees a woman blackout drunk and high
she can't see the future hurtling
towards her

and is like
bingo

you have no idea
how an apology might
change the story
I told myself then
and end the dream
I wake from
sweating out
your name

I would say that
if I could say anything

all these words
no one notices me
pointedly not saying

no one sees me drowning
with such intention
in the stream
of my deleted
tweets

                                        is it melodrama
                                        if you say nothing

I've had the experience
of both saying and not saying
and saying is better but

I follow one word
through to the next and then
suddenly I'm in the future
and I have no idea
where I am

sorry
but I can't review this manuscript
can't come to that event
can't leave my house
can't open my mouth
for "personal reasons"

don't read his tweets
don't read his
don't read
don't

do

                                        yeah but
                                easy for you to say

                                out there, not in here
                                where the past rushes in

                                        to remind me
                                there is no future

                                        coming for me
                                        just yesterday

                                shoving itself again and again
                                        down my throat

if you don't know you were my

(

i mean the cinematic,
for sure
way i know
the dread that seizes
hold of my breath
and holds there,
suspending time
until a half-memory
finds its way back
into my cells
and settles in
for another day
)

are you still my

maybe you're
nothing at all

just the pause at the end of the out-breath
held in a hammock
of absolute stillness
waiting for my signal
to swing out
towards anywhere

A TEAR HERE

There is a tear in her / She was torn / He tore her

a new universe
describes the known

surfaces that never seem
to change facts like

a tear / She, torn / He tore

galaxies so vast
and the direction always
down towards

theory
since city light
sings over
any possible

Tear in her / she / He

drips glitter
from space,

a cold somewhere
inside her,
hidden

Tear / her / his

undescribed motion
of the past

held captive
in the theatre of

Tear / here

speech
a length of stuttering light

O to unfurl
the throat at last
through

here / her

STILL, HERE

Just to be clear.

Maybe there is something underneath the sentence.
Some sentences lead you from one thought to the next, like a story.

But there is no story, no beginning-middle-end.

Meanwhile there is all this bubble and froth, these hitches.

A flashback isn't a memory, but an instance of time travel: the body believes it
is 1984, so a washing machine in a basement vibrates beneath your thighs, the
darkness in your limbs, coursing.

No matter how many times you go over this, it's not going to get any clearer.

This is what you did, later: you acted.

It felt like you came to the end of what you could endure.

So you took a break.

How many memories can one fit into the palm of now?

You recall thinking, repeatedly, *I will never forget any of this.*

In the schoolyard, eddying leaves.

Someone else's children gasping at sun through cherry blossoms.

Raucous laughter; you were in fact a funny drunk.

Five a.m. birds mocking your death wish.

There's a cup of tea cooling somewhere.

A spirited move towards safety, but the train's going by again, carrying zero ideas.

Every other phrase really means

It's nearly all gone.

The days are the days.

You convince M to sing to your belly, even though neither of you has any idea what the future holds.

You emit good cheer, honestly, but fail to document it.

Death is still waiting for you to stop rushing towards the next administrative task. Takes up his old place at the edge of the bed, hand on your chest, clocking each breath.

You enter every room
except the one with your name on it.

So you try following thought downstream, where it pools like milk in a bowl.

Is this whisper good to go, or shall we haul your voice into a wail again?

You take your pills.

It's a tangent plane, he explains again, and you ask again what that is.

You scrawl abstraction on the blank wall. With or without understanding, when you walk away it will hold itself up without the bother of you.

The dog or the kettle or the fire calls you to attention.

Death whispers his usual garbage.

You have messages waiting.

Response costs you nothing, and yet, most days, you refuse.

There's a dent in the wall of acceptance that you focus on for whole afternoons. Then, without warning, it descends like a blank wave—

It's still here.

Just when you think
the days are the days
and you are fully in them

this
thick film of *then*

settles now
as it always did

hands describe a tangent plane both *of*
and *against*

of and *against*
of and *against*
of and *against* and
if you can describe this it means you can

breathe through it

just like you did before

#STILLHERE

I am sad and I am walking

I am breathing and I am engulfed in flame

I am peripheral to your life and I am the centre of pain's harsh enterprise

I can't get out of bed and I am resting

I am a flash in the river and I am the spoiled salmon dinner

I am self-obsessed and I am a knot of winter afternoon light

#amwriting #amnotwriting

I am terror's own knot and I am barely a person

I am my own perfect disaster and I am in on the joke

I am completely out of fashion and I am still here

Notes

1. "Mind Map of the Rendered World" traces the path of the darkest night of my addicted life through dreams I later had in recovery.

2. "Coda" contains a quote from Gertrude Stein's *Tender Buttons*.

3. "The Big One: Field Notes" contains notes from my somatic therapy sessions with psychotherapist Anne Pepper.

4. "I Choose You" is based on both a dream and my experiences obsessively playing *Pokémon GO* in the summer of 2016.

5. "First Try or Failure," "There's Nothing There," "Try": As part of Margaret Christakos's Listen Deep event at University College, University of Toronto (March 8, 2019), I performed a collaborative, community-held ritual to bring the private experience of miscarriage into the public. While a chorus of voices performed "There's Nothing There," I transformed "First Try or Failure" into "Try." Thanks to Faith Arkorful, Julia Polyck-O'Neill, Evangeline Schram, Nikki Sheppy, Erin Soros and Jacqueline Valencia for voicing this transformation with me. The title "There's Nothing There" is a quote from an ultrasound technician upon observing my uterus.

6. "A Tear Here" was written for an issue of *Visual Verse* in response to an image by Mark Basarab: *visualverse.org/submissions/a-tear-here*.

Acknowledgments

These fine journals and anthologies first published the following poems, or earlier versions of them:

Arc Poetry Magazine 88 (Spring 2019): "An Internment"

Audeamus 2017 (Massey College): "Community Healing," "January"

Canada and Beyond: A Journal of Canadian Literary and Cultural Studies Vol. 7 (2018) (Universidad de Huelva, Spain): "Coda," "The Exact Nature of My Wrongs," "Following the Leader," "Mind Map of the Rendered World," "Two Truths and a Lie"

Hart House Review 25: "Forth," "Performance Anxiety"

NewPoetry.ca and *The Best Canadian Poetry in English, 2018* (Toronto: Tightrope Books): "Good God/Bad God"

POETRY (December 2017): "He Said She Said"

PRISM international 57.1 (Fall 2018): "Field Research"

The Puritan (Summer 2018): "Acknowledgments"

Visual Verse, Volume 5, Chapter 12: "A Tear Here"

Thank you to the editors.

Thanks to my editor, Shirarose Wilensky, for her generous attention and care with this book. Thanks also to Brian Lam, Cynara Geissler and Jazmin Welch at Arsenal for bringing this book into the world.

Thanks to Kimiko Murakami for being on standby. Thanks to Judah Murakami for ever-fresh perspectives. Thanks to Mary Jane for snoozing gently near my feet while I was writing this book.

Special thanks to Manfredi Maggiore for being my partner.

Dina Del Bucchia, Heather Curley, Elee Kraljii Gardiner, Angela Rawlings, Nikki Reimer, Erin Wunker and Daniel Zomparelli checked in on the regular. Thank you, friends.

My mother, Monika Murakami, passed away just after I finished this book, and then my child, Emilia, came into the world just a few days later. Thanks to my mother for the cookies. Thanks to Emilia for changing everything.

SACHIKO MURAKAMI is the author of three previous poetry collections, including *The Invisibility Exhibit* (shortlisted for the Governor General's Literary Award). As a literary worker, she has edited poetry, worked for trade organizations, hosted reading series, organized conferences, sat on juries and judged prizes. *sachikomurakami.com*